AF580185

Library of Shakespearean Biography and Criticism

I. PRIMARY REFERENCE WORKS ON SHAKESPEARE

II. CRITICISM AND INTERPRETATION

- A. Textual Treatises, Commentaries
- B. Treatment of Special Subjects
- C. Dramatic and Literary Art in Shakespeare

III. SHAKESPEARE AND HIS TIME

- A. General Treatises. Biography
- B. The Age of Shakespeare
- C. Authorship

Series III, Part A

'WHAT TO EXPECT OF SHAKESPEARE'

Library of Shakespearean Biography and Criticism

'What to expect of Shakespeare'

By

Jean J. Jusserand

BOOKS FOR LIBRARIES PRESS
FREEPORT, NEW YORK

First Published 1911
Reprinted 1970

INTERNATIONAL STANDARD BOOK NUMBER:
0-8369-5509-9

LIBRARY OF CONGRESS CATALOG CARD NUMBER:
70-128889

PRINTED IN THE UNITED STATES OF AMERICA

‘WHAT TO EXPECT OF SHAKESPEARE’

By J. J. JUSSERAND

July 5, 1911

It was the custom in former days that any one who addressed the French Academy for the first time should praise the great Cardinal, founder of that august body, and should compliment the king.

If similar customs prevailed in the British Academy, nothing would be easier for me than to comply with them. I should have to praise, I believe, as the ‘begetter’ of this new and already famous Assembly, the Royal Society; and to praise it as it deserves, it is enough to recall that it numbered among its Fellows, in its early days Newton, in its latter days Darwin.

No less easy and no less congenial would it be for me to compliment that Sailor-Prince, who reverently walked, a few days ago, to the foot of the altar in the Abbey where so many of his ancestors sleep their last sleep, and their great shades still keep watch over the nation. To him, the worthy inheritor of their best examples, have been handed down, with the crown, the traditions of a father whose ideal was peace with honour and with justice, and of a grandmother to whom it was given to break one of the oldest historical traditions of the British realm: the tradition that there could be no long English reign without a war with France. Hers was the first exception in eight centuries. May a foreign visitor be permitted to express the wish that the new reign, lasting as long as any that has gone before, shall transform the exception into the rule.

Addressing Queen Elizabeth in a year that is now famous, the year 1564, in which Shakespeare was born, Ronsard, speaking in the name of his then storm-ridden country, expressed that faith in its future which, at no period, has any French heart ever lost, adding that if it were possible to once join in a firm amity,

'Vostre Angleterre avecques nostre France,'

the Golden Age would return. If the Golden Age has not quite returned up to now, the cause is perhaps that the experiment has not yet been continued long enough. May it be long continued!

The theme assigned me by you is one which not even the boldest minds, the best informed, the most accessible to poetical beauty, dare approach without awe. Encouragement may, however, be taken from no less ardent a worshipper of the Shakespearian fame than Swinburne. 'For two hundred years at least,' did he write, 'have students of every kind put forth in every sort of boat, on a longer or a shorter voyage of research across the waters of that unsounded sea (the works of Shakespeare). From the paltriest fishing craft to such majestic galleys as were steered by Coleridge and by Goethe, each division of the fleet has done or has essayed its turn of work.'

For an occasion like the present no galley could be too great or too majestic. If it pleased you to select the merest fishing craft, the reason must be that, to come to you, it had to cross the ocean, and this doubtless humoured the fancy of a sporting nation. As soon, however, as your invitation reached me, I accepted it, thinking that the best courtesy was not to discuss but to obey, and considering that, for lack of better motives, my coming from the lands further away than 'vexed Bermoothes' was an homage I could offer which was not within the reach of many of my betters.

I

When Ronsard died at St. Cosme, near Tours, in December, 1585, Shakespeare being then twenty-one, all France went into mourning; besides the ceremonies at St. Cosme, solemn obsequies were celebrated at Paris, orations were delivered in French and in Latin by Cardinal Duperron and others; the crowd was such that princes and magnates had to be denied admission for lack of space; not one poet of note failed to express his sorrow for the national loss; these elegies were collected under the title of *Le Tombeau de Ronsard*.

On April 25, 1616, the bell of Holy Trinity Church at Stratford tolled, as we read in the register, for 'William Shakespeare, Gentleman', one of the chief men of the town, wealthy, good humoured, benevolent, known to have been somebody in the capital, and to have written very successful plays. A monument was raised to him with a florid inscription, such as is often granted to provincial celebrities. It was in fact a local event. 'No longer mourn for me,' the poet had written, 'when I am dead,'

> Then you shall hear the surly sullen bell
> Give warning to the world that I am fled
> From this vile world.

But the world knew nothing of it; the British capital paid no attention to it; not one line was written on the occasion, no poet mourned the event. 'At the passing of the greatest Elizabethan the Muse shed not one tear.'[1] When his plays were collected seven years after his death, they were preceded by a few eulogies, the authors whereof extolled his merits, but they went much beyond what they really thought, for they had to conform to the rules of the *genre*. The friends and fellow players of the author, who had edited the collection, apologetically offered 'these trifles' to two noblemen who had been pleased to think them 'something heretofore'. A second edition was only wanted nine years after the first, and a third only thirty-one years after the second.

What we see now needs no description. With the single exception of the Bible, no book has been in the same space of time the subject of such close studies and such ardent comments as the collection of 'trifles' first given to the world by Heminge and Condell in 1623. During the first five years of the present century twenty-seven new editions of Shakespeare's works were published; princes have played in his tragedies the part of princes, kings have tried their hands at translating his works. Some of his dramas have been played in Japanese; his *Julius Caesar* has been performed in the Roman theatre at Orange. His ideas, his sayings, the personages to whom he has given life, the scenes he has depicted, have become familiar to all; men born at the Antipodes will catch an allusion to a scene, a character, a word of Shakespeare's. By the middle of the last century the British Museum counted some three hundred entries under the word Shakespeare; it counts now more than five thousand.

A responsibility uncourted and unexpected by him weighs now on the poet. Books, like their authors, have their biography. They live their own lives. Some behave like honourable citizens of the world of thought, do good, propagate sound views, strengthen heart and courage, assuage, console, improve those men to whose hearths they

[1] Munro, *The Shakspere Allusion Book,* I. xiv.

have been invited. Others corrupt or debase, or else turn minds towards empty frivolities. In proportion to their fame, and to the degree of their perenniality is the good or evil that they do from century to century, eternal benefactors of mankind or deathless malefactors. Posted on the road followed by humanity, they help or destroy the passers-by; they deserve gratitude eternal, or levy the toll of some of our life's blood, leaving us weaker; highwaymen or good Samaritans. Some make themselves heard at once and continue to be listened to for ever; others fill the ears for one or two generations, and then begin an endless sleep; or, on the contrary, long silent or misunderstood, they awake from their torpor, and astonished mankind discovers with surprise long-concealed treasures like those trodden upon by the unwary visitor of unexplored ruins. No works are so familiar to the nations of the world as those of Shakespeare to-day. In their continued and increasing existence what sort of life are they leading?

In the course of ages, while praise and admiration were becoming boundless, an anxious note has been sounded from time to time, the more striking that it came from admirers. Two examples will be enough to make the point clear. While stating that 'the stream of time, which is continually washing the dissoluble fabrics of other poets, passes without injury by the adamant of Shakespeare', Dr. Johnson, who wanted his very dictionary to be morally useful through the examples selected by him for each word, stated that Shakespeare's 'first defect is that to which may be imputed most of the evils in books or in men. He sacrifices virtue to convenience, and is so much more careful to please than to instruct that he seems to write without any moral purpose . . . It is always a writer's duty to make the world better.'

Nearer our time, another, no enemy like Tolstoi, but a passionate admirer, Emerson, for whom Shakespeare was not *a* poet, but *the* poet, the 'representative' poet, wrote: 'And now, how stands the account of man with this bard and benefactor, when in solitude, shutting our ears to the reverberations of his fame, we seek to strike the balance? Solitude has austere lessons. . . . He converted the elements, which waited on his command, into entertainments. He was master of the revels to mankind. . . . As long as the question is of talent and mental power, the world of men has not his equal to show. But when the question is to life, and its materials, and its auxiliaries, how does it profit me? What does it signify? It is but a Twelfth Night, or Midsummer-Night's Dream, or a Winter Evening's Tale: what signifies another picture more or less?'

So spoke Emerson in one of those Essays which Matthew Arnold went so far as to describe as 'the most important work done in English prose in his century'.

What is it then that we possess? What can we expect of Shakespeare? Is the treasure in this bewitching garden of Hesperides mere glitter, or is it real gold? Do we listen to the seer that can solve our problems, answer our doubts, instruct our ignorance, soften our hearts, brace our courage? Or does the great book whose fame fills the world offer us mere revels, vain dreams and tales, no moral purpose, virtue sacrificed to convenience, such evanescent food as was served on Prospero's table for the unworthy?

II

Shortly after he had reached his majority Shakespeare came to London, very poor, having received but a grammar-school education, upheld by no protectors. The son of a tradesman, he reached the huge capital where one of his Stratford compatriots was established as a grocer, another as a printer. For some years he disappears, and when we hear of him again he is beginning to be known as an author. Having come to the city with no trade of his own, he had obviously soon discovered that he was better fitted to write plays than to sell groceries, and to compose books than to print them. He was apparently still in Stratford in 1585–6; six years later London dramatists are feeling jealous of the new play-mender or maker, five years after that he is a wealthy man, and purchases New Place, the finest house in Stratford, built by its most famous citizen, a former Lord Mayor of London. He was then thirty-three. Promptitude is the salient trait of such a career. When he died Shakespeare left thirty-seven plays; Racine only twelve.

Literary invention has been the subject in our days of minute research on the part of philosophers. Paulhan has shown what different roads lead to that supreme result, a memorable book of lasting fame. One road passes through the Elysian fields, another crosses the region made doleful by Tantalus, Ixion, and Sisyphus's ceaseless groans. For that modern dramatist Dumas *fils* the labour of literary composition was accompanied, according to Binet and Passy, by 'a great feeling of pleasure. While he writes he is in a better humour, he eats, drinks, and sleeps more; he feels a kind of physical enjoyment through the exercising of a physical function . . . Page after page in his manuscripts is without any erasure.'[1] Others, like Rousseau, or Flaubert, had a different tale to tell: 'My ideas,' wrote Rousseau, 'group themselves in my head with the most incredible difficulty: they move about obscurely, they ferment to the extent of upsetting me and giving me heart-beats, and in the midst of all that emotion I see nothing clearly; I could not write a single word, I must wait.' The same with Flaubert: 'I am in a rage without knowing why: my novel, maybe, is the cause. It does not come, all goes wrong; I am more tired than if I had mountains to bear; at times I could weep. . . . I have spent four hours without being able to write a phrase. . . . Oh, Art, Art, what is that mad chimera that bites our heart, and why?'

To the latter group most decidedly belongs Shakespeare's great rival, Ben Jonson. One must 'labour', said he sententiously; one must be 'laboured'; facility is the most dangerous of the Will-o'-the-wisps; it leads to bogs and marshes; do not follow Jack-o'-lanterns, bright as may be the lanterns; retrace your steps, 'The safest is to return to our judgement and handle over again those things the easiness of which might make them justly suspected.'

To the first class undoubtedly belonged Shakespeare. The number of his plays and the brief interval between the composition of each, two or three plays a year being his average production during the first eight years of his authorship, show that he must have written with the 'fine frenzy' attributed by his own Theseus to the gifted ones, flying 'an eagle flight, bold and forth on', like the poet in his own *Timon*. 'My manuscripts,' said Rousseau, 'are scratched, blotted, besmeared, illegible, testifying to the trouble they have given me.' Of Shakespeare, as is well known, his fellow players, who had seen him at work, said: 'What he thought he uttered with that easiness that we have scarce received from him a blot in his papers.' 'He never blotted out a line,' grumbled Jonson; 'would he had blotted a thousand!'

But he had other ways, and rather followed, to quote him again, his own 'free drift'. Why take so much trouble, when what he himself expected of his own plays could be reached without any of those Ixion-like agonies described by Rousseau and the others? For what he expected was simple enough, plain enough, and near at hand. What he expected he did actually attain, and his life was a successful life. His eye was on Stratford, not on posterity. His

[1] *Année Psychologique,* 1894, I. 79, 80.

dream was to end his days a well-to-do, respected citizen in his native town, and that dream was fulfilled. The idea of his being held later the Merlin of unborn times, the revealer of the unknown, the leader of men of thought and feeling, the life-giver, the pride of his country, never occurred to him, and would probably have made him laugh. His allusions to literary immortality in the *Sonnets* were only a way of speaking, which he had in common with the merest sonnet scribblers, as was well shown by Sir Sidney Lee; and since he never printed his, he cannot have cared much for an everlasting fame to be secured through them. For his poems proper he took some trouble; he published them; they were works of art; for his plays, a secondary *genre* in the common estimation, and in his, he took none; they were things of no import. He never printed any; a garbled text of some of the best was given, he did not care; silly plays were published under his name, he did not protest; he left no authentic text in view of a posterity which had never been in his thoughts; no books are mentioned in his will.

III

Literary fame as a dramatist troubled him not; but present necessities could not be forgotten; chief among them the necessity of pleasing his public. His average public, the one he had chiefly in view, whose average heart and mind he had to touch and delight, was that of the Globe, a large, much-frequented house which drew popular audiences, and where accidentally some Ambassador might appear; but the fate of the play would depend not upon the Ambassador's applause or some learned critic's blame, but on the impression of the crowd: a boisterous crowd, warm-hearted, full-blooded, of unbounded patriotism, a lover of extremes, now relishing the sight of tortures, now moved at the death of a fly, a lover of the improbable, of unexpected changes, of coarse buffooneries, quibbles, common witticisms easy to understand, of loud noises of any sort, bells, trumpets, cannon; men, all of them, of an encyclopaedic ignorance.

The part of such a public, as a contributor to Shakespeare's plays, can scarcely be over-estimated—a real contributor to whom it seems at times as if Shakespeare had passed on the pen to scribble as it pleased, or the chalk to draw sketches on the wall. What such people would like, and what they would tolerate, is what gave those plays which he never thought of after the performance, the unique, the marvellous, the portentous shape in which we find them. Great is the *de facto* responsibility of such a public; great that of Shakespeare too for having never denied it anything; great rather would that have been if he had not purposely intended to please only those living men, assembled in his theatre, on whom his own fortune depended; 'For we,' even Dr. Johnson had to acknowledge,

For we that live to please, must please to live.

From the writing of his plays, however, Shakespeare expected not one thing but two; first, immediate success with his public, and all that depended on it; second, the pleasant, happy, delightful satisfaction of a function of his brain duly exercised. This for us is the chief thing, what saved him in spite of himself: to the coarse food his groundlings wanted he added the ethereal food which has been for ages the relish of the greatest in mankind, while it had proved quite acceptable to his groundlings too. He added this as a supererogatory element because it was in him to do so, because it gave him no more trouble than to put in quibbles, jokes, or massacres, and because experience had shown him that, while it was not at all necessary to success, it did not hurt, and was received with a good grace. It was for him the exercise of a natural function, as it is for a good tree to produce good fruit.

Hence the strange nature of that work, touching all extremes, the model of all that should be aimed at, and of much that should be avoided; of actual use both ways. Prompt writing, as he had no choice (he had to live), the courting of a public whose acceptance of his work was indispensable, explain, with his prodigious, heaven-bestowed genius, how the best and the worst go together hand in hand in his plays, those flashes of a light that will never fade, and those concessions to the popular taste (indecencies, brutalities, mystifications, tortures, coarse jokes, over-well-explained complications), or the advantage so often taken by him of the fact that the public will not know, will not remember, will not mind. 'He omits,' says Dr. Johnson, 'opportunities of instructing or delighting which the train of his story seems to force upon him': the reason being that, in some cases, such opportunities did not occur to him at once and that he had little time for reconsidering; given his public, that would do. Hence also his anachronisms, his faulty geography, his indifference to real facts, so complete that he would not have stretched out his hand to take a book and verify the place of a city or the date of an event, nor would he have asked his future son-in-law whether a human being that has been smothered can still speak. He offers to his groundlings, and not to this learned age of which he never thought and which has no right to complain, a reign of King John without 'Magna Charta', but with plenty of gunpowder and with a Duke of Austria who was dead before the play begins. He adopts, for convenience sake, two rules to which none of his hearers could be tempted to object; one is, that all antique personages having lived in antiquity are, generally speaking, contemporaries and can quote one another, so Hector quotes Aristotle, Menenius talks of Alexander and of Galen, Titus Lartius compares Coriolanus to Cato. The other rule is that all distant towns are by the seaside. Rome, Florence, Milan, Mantua, Padua, Verona (to say nothing of Bohemia) are by the seaside. His personages go by sea from Padua to Pisa, from Verona to Milan; about to start from Verona they wait for the tide. Why take trouble? He wrote only for men who neither knew nor cared, composing plays not meant to survive and which had two authors, Shakespeare and the motley crew at the Globe.

IV

They have survived, however; their hold on the world increases as years pass, they are famous in regions the very name of which was unknown to their author. In the calm of our study, in the corner of a railway carriage, on the deck of a ship, we open the book and read the first scene of any play: Prospero's magic works on us; we are his, ready to follow him anywhere, to feel and believe as he tells us. The sight once seen, the words once heard, so impress themselves on our mind that the mere name of the place, of the man, woman, or child cannot be pronounced henceforth without the grand and lovely landscape, the loving, hating, laughing, weeping personage from the plays, and with him all that pertains to him, his family, his enemy, his friend, his house, his dog, appearing to us in as vivid a light as if he were here alive again, and we were pacing with him the terraces at Elsinore, the moonlit garden of the Capulets, the storm-ridden, witch-haunted heath of *Lear* or *Macbeth*, the woods near Athens, the forum at Rome, the enchanted park for an enchantress at Belmont, or the real battlefields where, in bloody conflict, France and England were shaping their destinies. So much life, such an intensity of realization are in the plays, that it is difficult to visit, in actual life, any of those places which Shakespeare sometimes merely named and did not describe, without the Shakespearian hero first appearing to us, before even we think of the real men famous there in times past. Grand or sweet figures, lovers whom death will sweep away, or leaders of armies, anxious Hamlet, scornful Coriolanus, loving Romeo, pensive Brutus, irrepressible Falstaff, and those daffodils of man's eternal spring—Portia, Rosalind, Ophelia, Juliet, Desdemona—rise bewitching, terrible, or laughable, at the mere sound of the words Elsinore, Eastcheap, Arden, Verona, Cyprus. So long as the mirage lasts our lives seem merged into theirs. Between the true artist and the product of his brain the phenomenon is a frequent one, but between the product of his brain and the readers of the book it much more rarely happens: 'A delightful thing it is,' said Flaubert in one of his rare happy moods, 'to write, to be no longer oneself, but to move through the whole creation one has called forth. To-day, for example, man and woman together, lover and mistress at the same time, I have ridden in a forest, during an autumnal afternoon, under yellow leaves; and I was the horses, the leaves, the wind, the words that were said, and the red sun that caused them to half close their eyelids bathed in love.' This privilege of the author, Shakespeare, for better, for worse, imparts to his listener or reader.

For better or for worse? Some of his worshippers, thereby courting protest and inviting injustice of an opposite sort, have dogmatized on his perfections, his omniscience, his prescience, the safe guidance he offers in every possible trouble, and the unimpeachable solution he propounds for every difficulty.

Wiser it is perhaps to acknowledge at once, with due deference to the purest intentions, that it is not exactly so. More than one of the gravest questions that, from the beginning, have troubled mankind would be put in vain to the poet, for to them he has no answer. What he does is to place the problem before us with such force that he obliges us to think seriously of those serious questions; hence of use, though of a different use than is sometimes said.

Concerning religions he does not take sides; as is evidenced by the fact that discussions are still renewed now and then (though there is little room for doubt) as to what faith he belonged to. The lesson he gives us is, however, a great one; it was a rare one in his day; and it is summed up in the word 'toleration'.

No problem is put oftener and more vividly before his audience than that of death and of the hereafter. To this he has no answer. In their calmest moods his personages hope for sleep: 'Our little life is rounded with a sleep.' Oftener he and they (he in the sonnets, they in the plays) pore over the prospect of physical dissolution, when the time shall come to leave 'this vile world, with vilest worms to dwell'. It seems as if for him as an author the apologue of the sparrow, told to King Eadwine by one of his Northumbrian chiefs, had been told in vain. We still 'go we know not where', and no Isabella, be she almost a nun, and bound by her part in the play to act as a consoler, has any word to clear her brother's doubts or ours. The attitude of Shakespeare, the writer, is that of the awe-inspiring genius whom Saint-Gaudens seated in Rock Creek cemetery, not of the one who carries upwards, from earth to heaven, the sacred flame of life in Bartholomé's monument.

As a patriot his teachings are mixed ones. Patriotism has two sides: it concerns our own country considered in itself, then our country considered in relation to others. The first kind of duty, the most natural and easiest, is admirably fulfilled by the warm-hearted, the sound, and thorough Englishman that the poet was, justly proud of the great deeds of glorious ancestors. His love is expressed in admirable lines for this 'dear, dear land':—

> This precious stone set in the silver sea,
> . . . .
> . . . that pale, that white-fac'd shore
> Whose foot spurns back the ocean's roaring,
> And coops from other lands her islanders.

As to the other side of patriotism, Shakespeare writes not only as a man of his day, but as a man who had to echo his public's feelings: an echo can make no change. To understand that, to picture the vanquished as a huge crew of cowards, traitors, and scoundrels, afraid of their own shadow, was *not* to increase the glory of a victory, proved beyond the reasoning capacity of the crowd at the Globe. The poet allows them to have their own way, to hold his pen, and write in his plays their own views of what an enemy must have been. They were his only care; unborn posterity and exacting critics that would come to life long after the plays were dead, as he thought, could have on him no influence.

On those great social problems which, in this modern world of ours, fill so much space in the thoughts of all, Shakespeare again expresses himself with the force and pregnancy of a man of incomparable genius; but he speaks as a man of his time and of his *milieu*, not as a man above them. The foibles of the masses, their credulity, their fickleness, their alternate fits of enthusiasm and depression, their aptitude to cruelty, their inability to understand, are depicted with the stern accuracy of a clear-eyed, unfriendly observer. The counterpart of such vices, or the extenuating circumstances resulting from involuntary ignorance, hardship, and misery are scarcely visible anywhere. The people, throughout the plays, are the same people, with the same faults, be they the Romans of *Coriolanus* or of *Caesar*, or the English of Jack Cade, or even the Danes of *Hamlet* (with their selection of Laertes for a king); they are the people. Shakespeare no more hesitates to offer them to the laugh and scorn of their brethren in the pit, than to-day's playwrights hesitate to ask a middle-class audience to laugh at the faults and folly of middle-class personages. The poet's lesson may be of use to statesmen, scarcely to the people themselves, since for a useful castigation the most valuable factor is love.

On one more question of keen, though less general, interest, we would appeal in vain to Shakespeare the playwright; that is for information about himself. Few men (I know that contrary views have been eloquently defended) have allowed less of their personality to appear in works dealing so directly with the human passions. Shakespeare's personality was of the least obtrusive; except in Stratford where he wanted to be, and succeeded in being, a personage, his natural disposition was to *keep aloof*. This general tendency is revealed by all we know about him. In an age and a *milieu* of quarrels, fights, literary and other disputes, he avoids all chances of coming to the front. 'His works,' said Dr. Johnson, 'support no opinion with argument, nor supply any faction with invectives.' The exceedingly curious discoveries of Prof. Wallace show us Shakespeare unwittingly thrown by events into a quarrel; his efforts to minimize his rôle and to withdraw and disappear are the most conspicuous trait in the new-found documents. The very reverse of his friend Jonson, who courted quarrels and shouted his opinion on all problems and all people, he carefully avoided every cause of trouble. As we know, he neither printed his dramas nor claimed or denied the authorship of any play; no writer in his day published his poems without laudatory lines from his friends; Shakespeare, keeping apart, never gave or requested any.

On rare occasions his persistence in expressing again and again certain views or feelings, or the casual inappropriateness of his personages' saying what they say, leave us no doubt that he adored music, loved the land of his birth, did not trust the mob, knew what a classical play was, objected to child-players, &c. These are exceptional occasions. The change we notice in the tone of his plays, as years pass, rather follows the curve of human life, of a life that might be almost any man's, than reveals individual peculiarities in their author. One of his chief characteristics (and merits) is, on the contrary, the free play he allows to his heroes' personality, and his care not to encumber them with his own. They go forth, fill the stage, fill the drama with their explanations and apologies, so freely, so unimpeded by the author, who seems simply to listen, that the spectator will at times remain in doubt which to believe and which to love. They pay no heed to Shakespeare, and they expound or contradict their maker's opinion without even knowing which. They are created independent and alive; they continue so to-day, the very reverse of so many characters in Hugo's dramas, mere spokesmen of the poet who wanted to imitate Shakespeare, but forgot to conceal, as his model had done, his own figure behind the scenes.

The *Sonnets* confirm these views; there alone Shakespeare's personality is, in a large measure, bared to the eye. But there the personage whose turn had come to speak was William Shakespeare, who used the same freedom that he had allowed to Shylock, Hamlet, Henry V, or Richard III. For him it was a kind of safety-valve, giving vent to sentiments which would have been out of place anywhere else; but it was enough for him to have put them down in writing; he did not go the length of sending the sonnets to the press.

V

Far above any of those single questions rises the one of general import, propounded by Dr. Johnson, Emerson, and others: that of the moral effect of the plays on listeners or readers.

During the whole period to which Shakespeare belongs, and before his day too and long after, in his country and out of it, most men agreed that plays must moralize and improve mankind. They have other *raisons d'être*, but this is the chief one. Tragedy and comedy, said Ronsard, are above all, 'didascaliques et enseignantes.' Sir Philip Sidney was of the same opinion. The true poet, said Ben Jonson, must be 'able to inform young men to all good discipline, inflame grown men to all great virtues, keep old men in their best and supreme state', and he deplored the debasement of that sacred rôle among his contemporaries, especially in dramatic poetry. According to Corneille the chief point is to paint virtue and vice just as they are; 'and then,' said he, with his austere optimism, 'virtue is sure to win all hearts even in misery, and vice is sure to be hated even triumphant.' 'The stage,' said Racine, 'should be a school where virtue would be taught no less than in the schools of philosophy.'

Samuel Johnson wrote his ill-fated *Irene* to show (but it turned out that no one wanted to see) 'how heaven supports the virtuous mind . . . what anguish racks the guilty breasts', and 'that peace from innocence must flow'; while Voltaire, for reasons of his own it is true, placed, in his *Babouc*, the moralizing influence of tragedies far above that of sermons.

The only shackles Shakespeare was loaded with were the needs and tastes of his public. They were heavy enough, but they were the only ones. The absence of others is so complete and so unique that this characteristic is among the most singular offered to our wonder by his works. Barring this single exception, no poet cast on the wide world a freer and clearer gaze. He wrote unhampered by traditions, rules, religious systems. He gave himself the pleasure of showing once that he knew dramatic rules existed, but he left them alone because they were 'caviare to the general', and he depended on 'the general'. They were probably, besides, not so very sweet to him either. The final result is that, strange as it may seem, he stands much nearer Aristotle than many of Aristotle's learned followers. The great philosopher did nothing but sum up the teachings of good sense and adapt them to Greek manners. The great poet did nothing but follow the same teachings, as given him by his own sound nature, and adapt them to English wants. As both were men of genius and both were excellent observers, the one taught and the other acted in similar fashion.

On the question of morality, Aristotle makes it quite evident that his own ideal is a drama in which vice is punished or even has no place; but he clearly states also that the rational end of dramatic poetry is not to moralize but to give pleasure (πρὸς ἡδονήν).

On the same question, as on that of 'rules' (mere suggestions, not 'rules' in Aristotle's intentions), Shakespeare's attitude was the same. He would not go out of his way either to secure or to avoid an ethical conclusion or conformity to rules. His plays were truly written 'without any moral purpose', that is, instruction was not their object. But to conclude that they do not therefore instruct at all is to wander from truth. First, in some plays the events represented are, as in real life, so full of meaning that the moral is no less obvious than in any classical tragedy with a confidant or a chorus to tell us what to think; and even, at times, the hero tells us that. No one can escape the lesson to be drawn from the fate of Macbeth, of Coriolanus, of Antony, of poor Falstaff and his wild companions. Augustus in *Cinna* does not moralize with greater effect on his past than does Macbeth:

Better be with the dead
Whom we, to gain our place, have sent to peace,
Than on the torture of the mind to lie
In restless ecstasy.

In many cases, however, it seems as if the evil power so often at play in Greek tragedies, and in real life too, were leading the innocent to their destruction: Othello, Desdemona, Hamlet, as worthy of pity as Oedipus; fatality imposing on them tasks for which nature has not armed them, or offering them temptations to which they would not have yielded had they been less generous. Are those plays of no moral use, or is their use limited to those maxims and pregnant sayings which Corneille considered one of the chief causes of a tragedy's usefulness, and which abound in Shakespeare—

'Tis time to fear when tyrants seem to kiss.

Great men may jest with Saints; 'tis wit in them,
But in the less, foul profanation—

and others so well known that one scarcely dares to quote them?

One instinct, and only one, appears in man at his birth, that of conservation. The child eats, sleeps, does what care for his growth commands, and can no more think of anything else than a tree can think of whether its roots absorb sap that ought to have gone to the next tree. What happens later is of immense interest: if too much of that native instinct persists and more than is strictly necessary for preservation survives, then the misshapen being solidifies into a low, mean, dry-hearted egoist. To call him with Stirner an ‘egotheist’ (*Homo sibi Deus*), to deify the monster, is only to make him more monstrous, and go back to the time when stones were deities. Hearts must open. ‘The aim,’ Lord Morley has written with truth, ‘both in public and private life, is to secure to the utmost possible extent the victory of the social feeling over self-love, or Altruism over Egoism.’ The chief influences will be inherited tendencies, family tuition, early examples. Next to that will be what and whom the growing man sees, hears, reads, associates with.

For compelling hearts to expand, and making us feel for others than ourselves, for breaking the crust of inborn egoism, Shakespeare has, among playwrights, no equal. Here works that supreme power of his: to bestow life, full and real life, on whomsoever he pleases, to delineate character with so great a perfection that such people as he presents to us we know thoroughly, and what happens to them strikes us the more since they are of our acquaintance; not a passing acquaintance, casually made, soon forgotten, but that of men who will accompany us through life, ever reappearing on the slightest occasion or merest allusion, in tears or smiles, moving us at the remembrance of a happiness and of disasters in which we take part though they be not ours. The action on the heart is the more telling that, with his wide sympathies, the poet discovers the sacred 'touch of nature' not only in great heroes, but in the humblest ones; not only in ideal heroines, but in a Shylock whom we pity, at times, to the point of not liking so completely the 'learned Doctor from Padua'; even in 'the poor beetle that we tread upon', and we get thinking of its pangs 'as great as when a giant dies'.

The fate of a Hamlet, an Ophelia, a Desdemona, an Othello, carries, to be sure, no concrete moral with it; the noblest, the purest, the most generous, sink into the dark abyss after agonizing tortures, and one can scarcely imagine what, being human, they should have avoided to escape their misery. Their story was undoubtedly written 'without any moral purpose', but not without any moral effect. It obliges human hearts to melt, it teaches them pity.

VI

Five thousand two hundred and sixteen entries to-day in the British Museum under the word Shakespeare (more than double the amount for Homer), against three hundred and seven in 1855; all the world reading Shakespeare: moral cannot be the only attraction, nor even the chief one. It is, in fact, as things of beauty that the works of the poet have reached their immense fame. That they are things of beauty is now admitted by all; with enthusiasm by most people, unwittingly by the rare others. Such a great writer as Tolstoi denies any merit, even of the lowest order, to Shakespeare, but having to define, in his book *On Art*, the tests by which 'real art' is to be distinguished from 'vain imitations', those he selects fit the works of Shakespeare so perfectly that, if this poet had been the typical one he had in view, he could scarcely have written otherwise.

Shakespeare's plays are things of beauty, works of art; the product of an art, it is true, which cannot be learned in books—the higher for that. What is then the use of a thing of beauty, an *As You Like It*, a *Midsummer Night's Dream*, full of smiles? and all that gaiety, and all that beauty, and all those passions, and that force, and that wit, and that eloquence, and that wisdom scattered through the immense field of the thirty-seven plays? 'What does it signify?' What should we expect of a thing of beauty?

No problem has been, for over a hundred years, more passionately discussed. Can art be profitable at all? Should it be profitable? Should it profit the few or the many? Is real art of a supra-terrestrial nature or not, and must it be kept above the reach and even the gaze of the lowly?

On these questions most critics have known no doubts, and they have answered without hesitation; but some have said, Certainly yes, and others, Certainly no. 'Woe,' wrote d'Alembert, 'to the artistic productions whose beauty is only for artists.' 'Here,' observed the Goncourt brothers, 'is one of the silliest things that was ever said.' The problem continues debated and debatable, and was quite recently the subject of a remarkable essay by one of the best Shakespearian critics: *Poetry for Poetry's Sake*, by Professor Bradley.

In the course of the last century the quarrel was at its height, and it was a fierce one. For a time no vocabulary had words strong enough to express the contempt, the hatred, the indignation of artists towards those unspeakable *bourgeois* who could imagine that art might be enjoyed by any but a select few, and could be of any use: 'Everything that is of any use is ugly,' Théophile Gautier had decreed. The true artist must live apart, meditate, never teach, never act: action might spoil the fineness of his perceptions. He belongs to a world different from everybody else's, the world of art.

But while literary wars and revolutions were going on, other wars and other revolutions were taking place in the world and deeply influencing art theories. The revolution of 1848 made of Baudelaire, that staunch champion of 'art for art', a convert to the opposite doctrine: 'Art is henceforth inseparable from usefulness and morality,' said he, burning what he had adored. The storm of 1870 thinned yet more the ranks of the erstwhile triumphant partisans of supra-terrestrial art. No doubt was possible, Browning was right,

> The world and life's too big to pass for a dream.

Since the din and dust of the fight have abated one can get a clearer vision of the facts; and as is often the case in human quarrels, one now discovers valuable truths, though in different proportions, in the doctrine of the contending parties.

The day of the pure dilettanti saying to the world, 'I am too much above thee to care for thee,'[1] is decidedly on the wane. Boutroux, with his usual acumen and sanity, has shown that their views, attitude,

[1] Cassagne, *L'Art pour l'art*, p. 143.

and success had never been a sign of progress, but of decay: 'In the epochs usually called epochs of decadence or dissolution, art disdainfully dissociates itself from any other object but beauty, considering that the latter displays its full power only when free from all accessory ends such as utility, truth, honesty, and is placed alone in its supreme independence and dignity.' Art is, in fact, an offspring of nature; it is of course in close alliance with beauty, but it must not be cut loose from the soil under pretence of mere beauty: 'Each time art has risen again from decay or has been born to a new life, it has begun by casting off vain ornaments and assigning to itself a serious and real end, closely connected with the conditions of contemporary life.'

But there is something true also in the theory of 'art for art'. If it cannot be maintained with Hegel, that art purifies all it touches, and that any kind of art is morally beneficial to mankind, it must be acknowledged to-day that art, when not wilfully perverse, is useful simply because it produces things of beauty. 'All that is great,' Goethe said, 'contributes to our education.' A tragedy, a picture, a statue; *Othello*, Rembrandt's philosopher, the Victory of Samothrace, raise us above ourselves. We cannot enjoy works of art, Paul Gaultier has observed, without 'a preliminary forgetting of our habitual preoccupations, and of the interested views which form, so to say, the woof of our lives. . . . They free us from the tyranny of interest. . . . The emotion caused by works of art acts like a preface to moral activity.' The same author adds with great truth: 'The morality of a work is not to be measured by the morality of the things represented, but by that of the sentiment in which they have been represented.'

The influence thus exerted will be powerful and beneficial, in proportion to the perfection of the work, the depth of the emotion, and the sincerity of the artist who takes his starting-point on our real earth, allowing himself to be prompted by our real lives and our real doubts and hopes. The influence will be broad in proportion to the accessibility of the beauty represented. Without those characteristics the kind of art that may grow will be short-lived, cold, and dry, the cult will not spread—few will worship nowadays a wooden idol.

Of the former sort is Shakespeare's influence on mankind. The world is full of beauty, but with our eyes drawn to the daily task most of it escapes us. We want the poet, the musician, the artist, to touch us with his wand and to say to us, Look. Then we see and admire what we had looked at a hundred times before, and never seen, owing to our 'muddy vesture of decay'.

A sunset may pass unobserved by the vulgar; it will less easily pass unobserved when arrested in its evanescence and fixed on his canvas by Claude Lorrain. For to the landscape is superadded Claude Lorrain; we have the landscape plus he; the artist changes nothing in what he sees, but he is present there with us, just to say, Look. The same with Shakespeare.

No sensible man visits that temple devoted to artistic beauty, with its innumerable recesses and shrines, where all epochs and all countries are represented, the Louvre in Paris, without leaving it a better man. The added worth may be an infinitesimal worth, it may be a considerable one; in all cases some worth will be acquired. Dormant springs of disinterested emotion will have been made to flow again, a fatigued brain will have been rested; sleepy thoughts will have been roused, brought back to life and made to engender others. The same after a visit to Shakespeare.

Private benefactors, or the State, offer to studious youths the means of making a stay in Rome or Athens, or of journeying around the world. The belief is that they will return stronger, better armed for life, having had unusual occasions to think and consider, to store their mind. Such journeys are offered us by Shakespeare, around that microcosm, so full of wonders, and which has no secret for him, man's soul and character.

His hold both on artists and on the masses will certainly continue; on artists on account of the example given by him of taking one's stand in realities, of looking at things straight, of observing nature rather than conforming to accepted traditions. This he does in absolute simplicity, without any touch of the pedantry of either the learned writer who worships rules because they are accepted, or the rebel who rejects them altogether, and on all occasions, because they are rules.

In Claude Lorrain's canvases we have nature, plus Claude Lorrain; in Shakespeare's plays we have nature, plus Shakespeare, plus his public. Discarding what is not his but has been contributed by his public, we find that what he adds to nature does not consist in any undue intrusion of his personality, but, on the contrary, in artistically selecting from real life what is characteristic of the individual he represents. One might follow, step by step, a Hamlet, a nurse, a Falstaff in real life and note every word they say, every attitude they take; and the portrait would be less life-like than the one drawn by Shakespeare. There are moments when we do not look like ourselves: such moments are often selected by photographers, for which cause so many photographs made after us are not like us. The true artist is more discerning; he not only keeps his own personality apart from that of his personages, but in that of his personages he knows how to bring out what makes of them distinct individuals. That is his way of saying, Look. Boswell's portrait of Dr. Johnson is immortal simply because it was drawn in that manner.

As a trammel-breaker, Shakespeare, who played a unique rôle in that French romantic movement, the chief result of which was the awakening of French lyricism—Shakespeare who was, said Emerson, 'the father of German literature'—will continue to help and inspire future generations of artists. Every successful new attempt usually degenerates into a school: to imitate the successful is ever held by the many as the shortest road to success. Old rules are periodically scorned and discarded; then, after a brief moment of independence, the new attempt (invariably made in the name of nature) is systematized, and new rules, new shackles, replace the former ones; barnacles retard the movement of the ship.

To look directly at nature; to see how Shakespeare looks at nature, to understand the amplitude of his realism, which does not, under pretence that nettles are real, discard roses; to read the parts of his plays which are really his, and study, for example, some of his wonderful first scenes (*Romeo*, *Othello*, *Hamlet*, *Tempest*, &c.), will be, on such occasions, the best of cures. Human nature will have to change before the great trammel-breaker ceases to fulfil his mission.

With the masses an increase of Shakespeare's influence is to be foreseen. His plays, in their *ensemble*, were ever accessible to the many, since it was for them especially that he wrote, but the higher beauties in his works, those which he put in simply because he could not help it, because they were commanded by his nature and not because they were required by that of his hearers, will be more and more understood and enjoyed.

The change in our own days has been striking; it will be greater hereafter, when owing to discoveries, to the improvement of machinery, to a change in the conditions of life, the many will at last enjoy that chief one among the great causes of content in life, which the few now possess and the masses do not—leisure hours. For the many, as for the privileged of previous times, life will be less encumbered with matter; there will be, in their day's twenty-four hours, time for rest, for study, for a friendly book, for thoughts. Instruction and education, kindly given as it will be (else of little advantage), will prepare them for the best use to be made of the new treasure with highest enjoyment and profit. Many, of course, as is often the case with the possessors of treasure, will squander theirs, but some will not, and their number will probably go on increasing. One of those highest enjoyments will be a better understanding of beauty, whether natural or artistic, a real sunset or a painted one.

Signs are not lacking that the influence for good of things of beauty, as such, will grow, and be more and more generally taken into account. A recent incident in far-off Colorado may be quoted as symptomatic. A commercial company there wanted, last year, to divert to its uses a stream which formed a cascade further down; it pleaded that it had, according to the Constitution, 'the right to divert waters of any natural stream unappropriated to beneficial uses.' Just as if it had taken its cue from Portia, the United States Circuit Court decided that 'The world delights in scenic beauty. . . . It is therefore held that the maintenance of the vegetation in Cascade Canyon by the flow and seepage and mist and spray of the stream and its falls, as it passes through the canyon, is a beneficial use of such waters within the meaning of the Constitution.' Thus, with the full support of public opinion, the stream was saved as being a thing of beauty, an honest one, and therefore beneficial.

The Palace at Versailles has been transformed, as you know, into a Museum dedicated 'A toutes les gloires de la France'. A visit there is for us what a reading of *Henry V* is for you. On Sundays the crowd is such that it is difficult to move: a crowd of the same sort that filled Shakespeare's theatre: artisans, shopkeepers, soldiers, sailors, servants, peasants come to town, and there too, now and then, a stray Ambassador. Such people are the best public, the most sincere, the one that does not look for occasions to blame and sneer, but occasions to admire, and few things are more beneficial than disinterested admiration for great deeds and noble sights. Leaving the palace once, at the hour of closure, I stood near a couple of obviously very poor and very tired people. They had been looking for hours, and they were gazing still. 'Now you must go,' repeated the Keeper for the second time. I wish I could render the tone and expression with which they answered: 'Must we now? What a pity. It was all so beautiful.' Like every man leaving with regret Shakespeare's works after having admired what is highest and truest in them, those two surely went home better people.

Let us not expect from Shakespeare what he cannot give, what he can is enough, and is of peerless value. Having come young to town, hard pressed by necessity, writing with very practical ends in view, never thinking of posterity, bound to please his public, the means of success he employed were in a way forced upon him by circumstances. He knew what ingredients his public liked, and never felt it his duty to grudge them their pleasure; he could write, and had to write, with extreme rapidity, without any preparatory study or verifying; and he did so without scruple. But no less fully did he allow free play to that unparalleled genius of his, the extent of which was unsuspected by his contemporaries and by himself.

By the problems he obliges us to consider, the concrete moral of some of his plays, their general healthy tone, the sympathies he awakens in our hearts, the amount of beauty he offers to our gaze, as varied as the world itself—by all this he renders us the one great service of drawing us out of our paltry selves, of busying us, not superficially, but intensely, with something other than our own interests. He raises us above the plane of everyday thoughts, he improves us by fighting in us the ever-recurring danger of our native egoism.

'How does it profit me?' Emerson had said; 'what does it signify? It is but a Twelfth Night, or Midsummer-Night's Dream, or a Winter Evening's Tale?' Let Emerson answer Emerson, for the same thinker had said elsewhere: 'All high beauty has a moral element in it.'